anxiety and me

Brief biblical thoughts to help
anxious believers

Guan Un

matthiasmedia
SYDNEY · YOUNGSTOWN

Matthias Media
(St Matthias Press Ltd ACN 067 558 365)
Email: info@matthiasmedia.com.au
Internet: www.matthiasmedia.com.au
Please visit our website for current postal and telephone contact information.

Matthias Media (USA)
Email: sales@matthiasmedia.com
Internet: www.matthiasmedia.com
Please visit our website for current postal and telephone contact information.

ISBN 978 1 925424 68 3

Cover design by Tina Nguyen.
Typesetting by Lankshear Design.

Contents

A prayer

If you're feeling anxious right now, try praying this prayer. Take your time. Pray it a few times if you need to.

Dear God,
You are good.
Your goodness is bigger than my anxiety.
And so I can be calm.
I can trust in you.
And we can have hope.
Amen.

The rest of this book is about why this prayer is true.

Introduction

My name's Guan and I have an anxiety disorder. That's not usually how I introduce myself at parties, but that's probably because I don't really go to parties, as I usually end up in the corner worrying about who I should talk to.

While this anxiety certainly isn't the only significant thing about me, it seems to be an enduring layer of who I am as a person. There have been times in my life when it's felt like I'm drowning inside my own head; when I've struggled to breathe because of the thoughts swirling like a whirlpool in my mind; when I've looked at the inside of my front door and known it was going to be too difficult to make it out the other side.

Anxiety can manifest in a lot of different ways—a restlessness, a circular worrying or thinking, insomnia, irritability, physical pain, or panic attacks. It is commonly linked with depression, or a generalized over-worrying or obsessive thinking.

If you're someone who doesn't struggle with anxiety (and *does* go to parties), you might ask, "How is anxiety as a disorder different from the general anxiety we feel—when work is stressful, or an exam is coming up?"

To put it simply: doesn't *everyone* have anxiety?

The short answer is yes: everyone will experience anxious periods, points in their lives that are more stressful or difficult, when we're uncertain about the future and what it will bring. Anxiety is a response to perceived danger. And there are points when anxiety is a *good* thing: when I see my child toddling towards a busy road, it's right for my brain to anticipate something going wrong in the future and jolt me into action.

But within that general category of anxiety is what is clinically called an anxiety *disorder*. It's when that anxiety is, in some sense, difficult to control—whether for biological, physiological, psychological, circumstantial, or relational reasons—and may start to interfere with your usual activities. Rather than being an obvious response to genuine danger, disordered anxiety may be a response to perceived danger that is unlikely to result in genuine harm, or is not perceived by others.

Here's an analogy: imagine you're in a car going down the highway—a multi-lane highway full of cars. The traffic is okay, so you're going at a decent speed— fast enough that you wouldn't want to stop suddenly.

Except you can hear something's wrong with the car. You try to change gears, and try again, but you're stuck in first. The car makes a terrible grinding noise as you try to shift the gearstick. And you can't get it unstuck by sheer force.

An anxiety disorder is a bit like having a broken gearbox. It's often combined with living a life that is going at high speed, or trying to keep up with people in the fast lane. Or it can be caused by something that has gone wrong in the past—like a difficult family background, relationship breakdown, or traumatic circumstances.

From the outside, it may not be obvious that someone has anxiety—that the gearbox is broken. Often, if they keep their foot down on the pedal, they can match speeds with the world around them for a while.

But on the inside, invisible to everyone else, are the grinding gears of anxiety. The motor is revving up to dangerous limits, which means something else might break if you don't find a way to get off the road and get the gearbox working again.

So the difference between this sort of anxiety and the common, everyday anxiety is a bit like the difference between a broken gearbox and the gearstick getting a little stuck as you're changing gears.

The first often requires external help. The second is situational and more fleeting.

I use the word 'anxiety' in this book to describe my own experience of having a moderate anxiety disorder and living day-by-day—and how God's word has helped me to do that. But, naturally, there is some crossover with general anxiety, and with other forms of anxiety—there are so many grey areas, it's impossible to separate them all completely (at least in a book of this length). And, as we'll see, I believe that what God's word offers is helpful in each of these circumstances—even though anxiety's most extreme forms may not be addressed here.

For the past ten years, I've been trying to think about what it means to have anxiety and to be Christian. And being a Christian wrestling with mental health in the modern world can be confusing, to say the least.

What I found I wanted, as I headed down the road with a broken gearbox, was a way to safely move off the highway. What I wanted in the depths of anxiety was a way to see light again.

And I found it in the psalms—specifically, one of the simplest and shortest of the psalms. I found answers that helped move me away from the edges of anxiety towards the comfort of the Lord.

A quick note: I'm writing this book primarily to those who themselves struggle with anxiety. But I hope it will also be useful to those seeking to understand more about anxiety, perhaps in order to care for those struggling with it.

Additionally, I'm writing this book as a follower of the Lord Jesus Christ for others who are trying to relate their Christian faith to what is going on inside them. If you don't yet know Jesus, I'm hoping this will still be useful to you while also helping you to understand the basis of Christian faith and hope.

A song against anxiety

Not all tools are the same.

Once, I was trying to take the screws out of a children's toy to replace the batteries. The screwdriver I had to hand was a little too big. It *almost* fitted, and would catch for a moment, and I'd try to force it and strip the screw a little bit more, get a bit more frustrated, and then repeat.

When I actually took the time to get up and go and get the right screwdriver for the job, the screws slipped out without a fuss.

This book is not an exhaustive look at every biblical reference to anxiety. If you're anxious, I suspect confronting you with a ream of Bible references would be using the wrong tool.

Rather, in the midst of anxiety, you may be able to

process something small and sharp, rather than something big and monolithic.

And in Psalm 131, one of the shortest psalms in the Bible, we find one of the Bible's shortest, sharpest answers to anxiety:

> O LORD, my heart is not lifted up;
> my eyes are not raised too high;
> I do not occupy myself with things
> too great and too marvellous for me.
> But I have calmed and quieted my soul,
> like a weaned child with its mother;
> like a weaned child is my soul within me.
>
> O Israel, hope in the LORD
> from this time forth and forevermore.

As you can see, Psalm 131 is just three verses long.

And yet, even though it's small, Psalm 131 contains three movements, one in each verse; three movements that help us move from anxiety towards the truths of the gospel.

In verse 1, God moves our heart from anxiety towards humility.

In verse 2, God moves our self from restlessness towards calm.

In verse 3, God moves our focus from our self towards others.

Let's have a look at verse 1.

From anxiety towards humility

Here are the statistics: according to an American study, more than a third of the US population (33.7%) will be affected by an anxiety disorder in their lifetime.[1] One estimate in 2017 put the global number of people with an anxiety disorder at 284 million, making it the world's most prevalent mental health disorder—and that was before the 2020 pandemic hit.[2] The latest mental health survey in Australia, where I live, says that one quarter of Australians have experienced an anxiety disorder.[3]

Take a moment to think about that, not in terms of statistics but in terms of the *people* you know. That would mean one person in each row of seats at your church; one or two people in each Bible study group; one person in each family with an average number of kids.

And while it seems like a very modern disorder, Danish philosopher Søren Kierkegaard wrote about anxiety way back in 1844, calling it the "dizziness of freedom".

What he meant was that anxiety is brought about by choice—without freedom and without choices, maybe we wouldn't have anxiety.[4] Kierkegaard didn't think of anxiety as negative. Rather, he saw "dizziness" as the cost of having consequences for your choices. It reminds you that you can use your choices for better or for worse.

But I suspect that even Kierkegaard couldn't have predicted the age we live in: a world overflowing with choices. After all, what we often think of as freedom is about choices and what we get to choose.

Let's say that you're one of the many people who check social media on their phones when they wake up. Suddenly, seconds after waking, you're faced with choices: do you like this post or comment? Do you ignore it? Do you post something yourself? Do you RSVP to that event or not bother?

Before you've got out of bed, you've had to make thirty or forty micro-decisions. I'm not saying this to dunk on social media, but simply to point out that this is a scale of decision-making that was unknown in Kierkegaard's day, or even twenty-five years ago. (Although, as an aside, I suspect social media is poisonous for those with anxiety for a whole range of reasons.)

Each of these choices might not seem significant

or anxiety-producing in itself, but we live in a world where our decisions are multiplying at an alarming rate. When I go to buy jeans, I can choose the width and length and cut (skinny or slim or straight or boot or taper or athletic or regular), the colour, the style, and the precise number of pre-ripped holes that make them seem like they're worn in.[5] When I'm booking a holiday and trying to work out where to stay, I can choose between a hotel or a resort or an Airbnb, and sift through thousands of reviews of hundreds of options for each night of my trip.

There are certainly good things about having this unprecedented freedom and choice. But what we don't often notice is that each choice between two or two hundred things makes you ask another question: "Which one is better?" And that drives another question: "What criteria am I using to make my choice?" Is it about the value for money, or the experience that I'm going to get? Is it about my comfort, or the adventure? Is it about the ethics of where my money goes, or the wisdom of spending less money?

If you have an anxiety disorder, each question becomes more fraught and can spawn a host of other questions in its wake. And so we try to take control of our lives by answering all these questions, but we're left dizzied.

In all of this, facing question after question, we feel the "dizziness of freedom". And it might seem impossible to find safe ground to rest upon.

But notice where Psalm 131 begins:

O LORD, my heart is not lifted up;
   my eyes are not raised too high;
I do not occupy myself with things
   too great and too marvellous for me. (v. 1)

If I was writing this psalm, I'd say something like: "I do not concern myself with the things that I don't understand. I won't bother with the things that I don't know."

But David, in writing the psalm, says something different. He writes: "I do not occupy myself with things too great *and too marvellous* for me". The word 'marvellous' here is not a synonym for 'amazing'. It can also mean 'difficult'—the Holman Christian Standard Bible puts it this way: "I do not get involved with things too great or too difficult for me."

When we see a night sky filled from edge to edge with star after star, or we feel the soft touch of a new-born child; when we see the ocean cover the horizon and the waves crash against the shore, or we climb to a height to look out over an expanse of nature—all these things remind us of how much happens beyond our control and outside our understanding. And the only right reaction is wonder and humility, knowing how far we are from accomplishing such things by our own hands.

That is why Psalm 131 answers anxiety with humility—"my heart is not lifted up". That is the safe ground that says there are things outside my control and outside my reach, and that is *good*.

How can we be okay with things being out of control? Why isn't David more concerned?

The simple answer is because he knows God is good.

I know that seems like the simplest of Sunday school answers, but here's what it means: in my anxiety, as I wrestle with my decisions and what they all mean, and as I whirl around in the "dizziness of freedom", and as I try to play God over my own part of the world, the psalm tells me to stop and look outside myself.

One of the constant, niggling questions that anxiety asks is: "How can I do all of this by myself?"

The answer the world gives is that "You can do it by yourself!" And the world suggests in constant, subtle ways that everyone else is managing just fine. And maybe, if you find the magic bullet, read the right book, or just buckle down and work harder, you too can assemble all your stuff into some sort of meaning for your life. "You can do it!"

But the gospel gives a different answer: "You can't do it—but that's okay, because you're not supposed to do it all by yourself." You *can't* do it all by yourself because *you're not meant to*. You weren't made to do it all.

Sometimes my kids try to be helpful (emphasis on *sometimes*). On one holiday, as I was carrying things downstairs to load the car, my then six-year-old said,

"I can help", and rushed in to take a suitcase. The problem was that the suitcase was adult-sized and heavy—it was simply too much for her. She tottered under the weight of it for a few steps, determined to do it herself, while I was right there, ready to take it from her.

Our psalm reminds me of how often I act as if I can do it on my own, struggling to take the weight of the things that I believe are in my control while God is waiting to take the load.

I act as if I am God over my domain, as if I have complete control over all these decisions and choices and outcomes, when the God of creation is standing next to me running the universe—a universe that includes the domain I think I control.

And we have a word for God's willingness to take the load: *grace*.

Grace is the shortcut to the biblical idea that nothing of what we have—especially the new life that is ours in Jesus—is because we have earned it. Nothing of what we do, no earthly merit, no work of our hands, could earn what God gives us freely, because Jesus died for us.

And grace meets our anxiety head-on. Grace means that we can look outside ourselves and see that within and beyond our domain, within and beyond our anxieties, bigger than all the things that we can control, is the God who is in control of everything.

This is the God who shaped the stars and fashioned the Milky Way—the God who keeps every atom vibrating and every heart beating. This is one way that David knew God was good: "The heavens declare the glory of God, and the sky above proclaims his handiwork" (Ps 19:1).

And even better than that? He's the God who knows you: knows every hair of your head, every beat of your heart, every depth of your despair and every edge of your anxiety. And he is willing to take the load.

In anxiety, it is good to humbly realize that there are things not in our control—because God is in control, and he is good. And it is good to realize there are things we do not and cannot know—because God knows, and he is good.

The wonderful and infinite goodness of God is greater than our anxiety, and that should give us pause and lead us to a humble quietness—just as in the psalm:

O LORD, my heart is not lifted up;
    my eyes are not raised too high;
I do not occupy myself with things
    too great and too marvellous for me. (v. 1)

From restlessness towards calm

But I have calmed and quieted my soul,
   like a weaned child with its mother;
   like a weaned child is my soul within me.
   (Ps 131:2)

Now, it might shock you for me to say this, but there's something about Psalm 131 that you might not have noticed yet. Did you notice that verse 2 comes *after* verse 1?

I know you might need a moment to sit down and take a few deep breaths after that groundbreaking insight.

But my point is that you can't skip ahead.

You see, it's possible that when you read these verses, you saw the verse about stilling the soul and assumed that's what this book is about. Maybe you thought, "Why don't we just cut to the chase and get straight to that verse?"

But verse 2 comes *after* verse 1. You don't get to the calm of verse 2 without the quiet of verse 1—the quiet that comes from humility. When we pause to see that the goodness of God is greater even than the reach of our anxieties—when we have humbled ourselves to that great truth—then this is where we arrive:

I have calmed and quieted my soul,
    like a weaned child with its mother.

You don't have to know much about babies to know that a newborn is *not* a picture of calm. She can be when she is sleeping, but when she is hungry or cold or uncomfortable or has a dirty nappy or any of the other baby things go wrong, she is not calm. And she will let you know about her current lack of calm in the only way she can.

This is especially the case if she's with her mum, who might be trying to calm her by rocking her to sleep. But the baby can sense her dinner, in the form of mother's milk, nearby. And so she'll let her mum know about her lack of calm by crying. Loudly.

But a weaned child has grown to a stage where she doesn't need milk from her mother any more. She's not going to cry about what her mother isn't providing. She can stay calm. She's free—free to enjoy the safeness and contentment that she can only find in her mother's arms. That is the picture of contentment—

the peace—portrayed in this psalm.

But how do we find this peace? Our first clue is in verse 1—that context where we realize that God's goodness is bigger than our anxieties. We go through the quiet to get to the calm.

Our second clue is in Christian meditation.

Meditation has a growing reputation in our wider culture as something that can be a welcome antidote to the busyness of life. Remember our analogy of being stuck in first gear on the highway? Meditation can be helpful for getting the car off the highway and fixing the gearbox. It's a way of relaxing the brain and attending to the body, which can be a useful remedy when our minds feel out of control.

But this verse shows us the difference between *Christian* meditation and other types of meditation.

Other kinds of meditation are about detaching yourself from the situation and saying that you are in the centre, and you are in control of that situation.

Christian meditation is different. It's about centring yourself in the knowledge and love of God; being with him, like a weaned child with its mother, safe in the knowledge that he is in control of everything.

Other kinds of meditation are about distance: they say that what you're going through doesn't matter all that much, and they ask you to empty your mind.

Christian meditation is about reminding yourself that *you* matter—so much that God sent his Son to die for you—and filling your mind with his promises:

that he will never leave you or forsake you; that his love for you is eternal, complete, and unending; that he has prepared a home for you, free from anxiety.[6]

Other kinds of meditation are about letting go.

Christian meditation is about *holding on*—holding on to the extraordinary love of the Father and trusting in how lovingly he holds on to you in his love, mercy, and grace.

By meditation, I don't mean that you must ring a bell or chant a mantra. But the reality is that finding a place and space to be quiet and remind yourself of the love that the Father has for you is helpful—and that's really the heart of Christian meditation. And doing that regularly is a good thing for everybody—especially those who suffer from anxiety. It can be especially good to find physical space, like a bushwalk or a place to swim, a café, or even putting on headphones at home.

Even when that's difficult, you can make spiritual space for yourself. Listening to God's word or to spiritual songs, or using apps to remind you to pray or to read a small part of the Bible—all of these are things that can help you in anxious moments.

One thing I've found particularly helpful in anxious times is to write a prayer—a short one (like the one at the start of this book) that puts my anxiety before God and reminds me of his love. I then use this prayer as a wallpaper on my phone, as a quick and simple go-to for when I feel stressed, to try and short-circuit the anxious cycles that would otherwise run through my mind.

Another option is to hide a small part of God's word inside yourself, something that you memorize in easier times for when things are hard. It might be a verse that reminds you of his great love or promises: perhaps John 14:2, 1 John 4:9-10, Psalm 23, Romans 8:38-39, or, of course, Psalm 131 itself.

But there's a third clue here about how to find contentment and peace. Verse 2 of our psalm talks not only about the peace that we can have in our self, but about the relationship that we have with our self: how we view our self and treat our self in our mind.

One way to see this is in our 'self-talk'. 'Self-talk' can be defined as the story that plays on repeat in your brain. It's the story in which you are the main character, but in which the narrative itself almost inevitably becomes a bit warped. Everything that you do or say or think becomes a part of that story. There's often a feedback loop where the things that happen in the story reinforce particular themes, and particular narratives come to the fore again and again. Things from your childhood, especially to do with shame or guilt, often become strong themes for your self-talk story.

For example, I used to work with a woman who was a model employee. She was industrious and smart, brilliant at communicating what needed to be done, and always on top of all the various responsibilities of her job. She was a pleasure to work with, and her performance reviews were glowing.

But once, in conversation with her, I made a passing comment about how hard she was working. Her eyes went somewhere else, and she waved her hand dismissively and said, "No, I'm just a lazy person".

What astounded me was that the *last* thing anybody else would have said about her was the *first* thing that she said about herself. That was her self-talk emerging, a part of her story that had become embedded in her mind, at some point in her life, and left to play on repeat.

That kind of self-talk is not easy to change. Because it plays on a constant loop in the background of our brains, we have often had thousands of hours of practice at believing the wrong thing about ourselves.

For those with anxiety, that self-talk often plays stories in the key of "you should" or "you have to" or "you must":

> "You should be doing more."
>
> "You have to get this under control."
>
> "You have to make sure you're not letting anyone down."
>
> "You must not be lazy."
>
> "You must not fail."

And sometimes, that self-talk has a sting in the tail:

> "You *must* do better... or you'll be a failure."
>
> "You *must* have control... or it's all going to go wrong *again*."

If we shine the light of the gospel onto those stories, we find that we say things in our self-talk that we would never say to someone else.

Imagine if, after church, a friend accidentally drops his coffee cup, and it shatters. And then imagine I respond by shouting at him that he is a worthless person who needs to work harder, otherwise he is going to be a complete failure, and everyone will know what a failure he is. Hopefully, I wouldn't get very far before someone stopped me and rebuked me.

But if I say similar things to myself in my own head and call it 'self-motivation', nobody else can see or hear it for the lie that it is.

The beauty of verse 2 of our psalm is that as it moves us from restlessness to calm, we have the space and opportunity to see that self-talk—the story in our heads—for what it really is.

God frees us to slowly change the words of that story—from:

> "You should be doing more" to "Jesus has done it all."
>
> "You have to get this under control" to "God has all things in his hands."
>
> "You have to make sure you're not letting anyone down" to "You are saved by grace alone."
>
> "You must not be lazy" to "You are loved no matter what you do."

"You must not fail" to "You are accepted no matter how you fail."

This is part of the work of the Holy Spirit within us. As the Spirit speaks, we catch glimpses of ourselves not as we *think* we should be, but as we *are*: completely loved, fully accepted, freely forgiven children of God. Changing our self-talk is not easy, but we have the greatest force in the universe helping us to become free: "The Spirit himself bears witness with our spirit that we are children of God" (Rom 8:16).

Please don't hear me saying that this verse in the psalm is the silver bullet that will make your anxiety disappear. If the gearbox is broken, then you need to take steps to get it fixed. And this might be something you need repeatedly as life goes on, or occasionally, depending on circumstance and life stage. In my case, seeing a doctor and a counsellor, praying with a faithful Christian minister, and praying with friends have all been important. They have been important ways of caring for my self.

And yet, as often as you need it, this is what the psalm tells us: that we can move from anxiety to humility, and from restlessness to calm. The psalm reminds us that because God is who he is, we can be still and know that he is God. And we can do so in a way that changes our self-talk from who we *think* we should be to who we *are* before the Lord.

But it doesn't end there.

From our self towards others

> O Israel, hope in the LORD
>> from this time forth and forevermore.
>> (Ps 131:3)

In comparison with the previous two verses, this verse might not seem worth talking about. Maybe your eyes glanced right past it. Or maybe you figured it was a rote ending to the psalm, in the same way that we end emails with 'Kind regards', or a prayer with 'Amen', or a text message with an emoji.

But it's more than that. Here, too, there is a movement—from our self out to others. Here, David is asking those around him to put their hope in God.

When you're in anxiety, it's tempting to think that there's nothing you can do for others. The story anxiety tells you is that you are alone, that you have to do everything yourself, that nobody else will help you. But anxiety might also tell you how hard that is—that you can't carry your own burdens, let alone anyone else's. And this story can go around and around without end.

Let me illustrate.

Sometimes, on a Sunday, when I think about going to church, I get anxious. My family goes to a church that we love: it's warm and welcoming, and it has a caring and engaged staff team. It's a place where people love Jesus deeply and thoughtfully. And we have brothers and sisters there who love us with grace and forgiveness.

And yet, despite all that, anxiety finds a way to creep in as Sunday morning approaches.

I think about what I'm going to say, and who I'm going to say it to. I think about whether that person really likes me or is just being polite. I think about whether we're doing enough as a church. I think about whether we're doing too much as a church. I think about people who haven't been there in a while. I think about the people who are in the valley of darkness in one way or another.

And sometimes it's a struggle to make it out the door.

But when I arrive at church, and I start talking to people, and I listen to how other people are doing, and I pray and sing about the God who sent his Son to die for me, and the service and the sermon help me once again to consider the cross and how Jesus died for me, and that this startling truth remains true forever—well, that's a very different story from the story that anxiety tells me.

I'm not saying this happens every time I go to church, or that to get rid of anxiety all you have to do is go to church. That's far too simplistic. What I am saying is that sometimes when we serve others, the intense inward spotlight of anxiety moves outward. The internal story that 'you have to do this alone' is eroded when you love someone else. I think this is part of the reality of Colossians 3:1-3: in church, we are reminded to "seek the things that are above", and we are reminded that "[our] life is hidden with Christ in God".

And I suspect the writer to the Hebrews knew this when he reminded his readers that they should be "not neglecting to meet together, as is the habit of some, but encouraging one another, and all the more as you see the Day drawing near" (Heb 10:25).

This is not the same as somebody trying to combat anxiety with busyness, or saying "Just pull up your socks and get on with things" (or "Get to church"). But being in the presence of a group of believers who have hope—who have looked outside themselves, who love and trust God, who care for each other—helps to negate the relentless inward self-focus of anxiety.

And more than that, it reminds us that those with anxiety have something that they can bring to others:

a reminder of hope in the Lord.

Old Testament scholar Robert Alter suggests that in Psalm 131:3, the "quiet contentment of the speaker is being proposed as a model for how a trusting Israel should wait for the LORD".[7] That is, in this verse, the psalm moves from inward to outward, from individual to community.

And how much more so for us who live in the knowledge of God's full revelation in Jesus. We have seen the full display of his love and care for us, because we can see what Jesus has done for us on the cross. We have the full picture of where our hope lies.

Ponder for a moment how anxiety tempts us to think that it is what we're doing that matters. And not only that, but how well we're doing it, and how much of it we're doing.

But the movement of Psalm 131 reminds us that contentment and assurance matter more than doing. Like Martha in the story of Mary and Martha (Luke 10:38-42), we are reminded to value the presence of God over busyness, peace with God over restlessness, and contentment in God over insecurity.

As we saw previously, this is not an 'inner peace' kind of contentment, but the real contentment of knowing that God the Father, the Creator and Lord, knows you, and dwells with you, and is at peace with you.

Sometimes, hope can be hard to see. It is a little bit less tangible for someone who hasn't been through the valley of suffering. You might talk about the hope of heaven to someone who has lived a comfortable life, and they might say, "Yeah okay, that sounds pretty good. That sounds a little bit better than what I have here."

But the hope of the gospel becomes more clearly defined, easier to grasp and cherish, when offered to those struggling with anxiety—or depression or body image or chronic illness, or any of the other myriad things that we struggle with in this world.

Hope becomes more real when we can offer it to those in the valley. It becomes more real when we can say to someone who is struggling with the guilt of their own self-doubt, "One day, you will see God face to face. One day, you will come to the place where you no longer have to lower your eyes before his goodness. One day, you will come to the place where we can lift our faces to see his glory and drink it all in."

The place where there is no anxiety. The place where there is nothing to be anxious about because every part of us is at peace.

When we can talk about those things, there is hope.

When you have personally come through the valley, the best thing is not to camp there on the edge, but to take other people through the journey you have experienced. This is how Paul puts it: "If we are afflicted, it is for your comfort and salvation; and if we are comforted, it is for your comfort" (2 Cor 1:6). For Paul, God's comfort doesn't remain static, but moves outward as a gift to others.

If someone has never been in the midst of the valley, you can remind them that the valley exists. And if someone is in the midst of the valley, you can remind them that there is a way out.

And for those struggling through anxiety, your hope might remind them that they are not alone, and that others have come through it. Your hope might remind them to not become a victim; to not let the darkness define who they are.

Of course, there may be other valleys in your journey, but for now: "hope in the LORD".

God, anxiety and you

There's a TV comedy sketch from the 90s that goes something like this.

A woman goes into a psychologist's office and introduces herself to the man behind the desk. The man tells her about his unusual pricing structure: he charges $5 for the first five minutes, and then nothing else, because his sessions never last that long. The woman is surprised, but happily agrees.

The man says, "Tell me about the problem".

The woman says, "Well, I have this fear of being buried alive in a box. I think about it and begin to panic. I can't go through tunnels, or be in an elevator —anything boxy."

The man says, "Well, I'm going to say two words to you right now, and I want you to listen to them very carefully. And then incorporate them into your life."

The woman is a little surprised, but agrees.

The man leans forward and shouts at her: "Stop it!"

It's a simple sketch (and probably funnier to watch than to read in explanation) but, like many comedy sketches, I think it gets to a truth that can be otherwise difficult to describe. On one level, we know the "Stop it!" solution doesn't work (anxiety and other mental health disorders run deeper than the level at which we can choose to stop)—and yet there is a part of us that wants it to be that simple. We see someone in the pain of anxiety, and part of us may want to shout, "Stop it!"

But there's a Christian version of "Stop it!" as well, where we simplistically label all anxiety as sin—and tell a brother or sister to, well, "Stop it!"

To be clear, some forms of anxiety may be sin. As we saw in the chapter about verse 1 of our psalm, sometimes we can fail to trust God to carry the burden. Sometimes a sin-filled world will give us things to be anxious about. Sometimes anxiety will emerge because of our finite understanding of the situations we're in—and of what God may be doing in all the circumstances of our lives.

But sometimes, as well, the sins of others can cause a trauma that creates an internal anxiety, which becomes very difficult to unearth apart from professional help—and nearly impossible to 'choose' not to experience.

And so, while some types of anxiety are bound up

with sin—and so should rightly be approached with (slow, patient) repentance and with renewed faith in God—the larger issue is far more complicated.

In the end, I think the Bible gives us a much better answer than "Stop it!"

One of the most-quoted New Testament verses about anxiety comes from Philippians 4:4-7, especially verse 6:

> Rejoice in the Lord always; again I will say,
> rejoice. Let your reasonableness be known to
> everyone. The Lord is at hand; *do not be anxious*
> *about anything*, but in everything by prayer and
> supplication with thanksgiving let your requests
> be made known to God. And the peace of God,
> which surpasses all understanding, will guard
> your hearts and your minds in Christ Jesus.

Let's think about the context. This letter comes from Paul as he expresses his love for and fellowship with the church in Philippi: "my brothers, whom I love and long for, my joy and crown... my beloved" (4:1). He then urges two women, Euodia and Syntyche, to "agree in the Lord" as his "fellow workers" and labourers in the gospel. Paul doesn't 'shout' at them about anxiety, but encourages them, in the context of a loving relationship, to see the God who listens to our prayers, and to notice the abundant and unsurpassed peace that Jesus has won for them.

Within that relationship between Euodia and

Syntyche, there has been some sort of fracture—we don't know what it is, but it's big enough for Paul to address in his letter. In that context, his message in verse 6 is less a sharp warning against anxiety ("Stop it!"), and more a reminder of how God can bring about relational change—how, in prayer, that anxious state of friction with another person can be healed, and how God provides a better alternative than anxiety: in rejoicing, in thanksgiving, in prayer, and in understanding the peace that Jesus brings.

The other place we might turn is the famous passage in Matthew 6, part of the Sermon on the Mount:

> "Therefore I tell you, do not be anxious about your life, what you will eat or what you will drink, nor about your body, what you will put on. Is not life more than food, and the body more than clothing? Look at the birds of the air: they neither sow nor reap nor gather into barns, and yet your heavenly Father feeds them. Are you not of more value than they? And which of you by being anxious can add a single hour to his span of life? And why are you anxious about clothing? Consider the lilies of the field, how they grow: they neither toil nor spin, yet I tell you, even Solomon in all his glory was not arrayed like one of these." (Matt 6:25-29)

Again, notice that this is not a direct or simplistic confrontation, but a reminder of our greater circumstance: of the Creator God who cares for all his created things, of the beauty of creation, of the generosity of the God who arrays the flowers with colour and equips the birds with song. And of the God who cherishes you far above all these things.

More than this, Jesus knows us inside and out. He knows our anxieties and our hopes, our fears and our dreams. And he does not shout at us to "Stop it!" but walks with us in all these things. Hebrews 4:15-16 reminds us:

> For we do not have a high priest who is unable to sympathize with our weaknesses, but one who in every respect has been tempted as we are, yet without sin. Let us then with confidence draw near to the throne of grace, that we may receive mercy and find grace to help in time of need.

But above all, we can see the Bible's response to anxiety in Jesus, in the garden of Gethsemane, knowing he is going to the cross. While not dealing with a disorder, he is clearly overwhelmed with anxiety: "My soul is very sorrowful, even to death; remain here, and watch with me" (Matt 26:38). And yet he remains faithful, sinless, and prayerful in the face of all that he is about to encounter—even compassionate to the disciples who slept on their watch.

He knows that he can be faithful because he, above all, knows who God is. The God who wants us to bring all our anxieties *to* him, because he cares for us (1 Pet 5:7). The God who has given us the Spirit of adoption, by which we can call to him as Father (Rom 8:15). The God of comfort, "who comforts us in all our affliction, so that we may be able to comfort those who are in any affliction, with the comfort with which we ourselves are comforted by God" (2 Cor 1:4).

In all the depths of our anxiety, God does not rebuke, or threaten, or shout at us to "Stop it!"

But this is what God says to us in Jesus: "Come to me, all who labour and are heavy laden, and I will give you rest" (Matt 11:28). This is the God we can put our hope in.

Hope in Christ

But there's one more thing. It's all very well to say, "Put your hope in the Lord", but how do you do that?

After all, being in anxiety is almost the opposite of hope. When you're in an anxious panic, part of the problem is that you're not able to hope. You're not able to see the outcomes or the solutions.

In moments like that, I'm reminded of 1 Peter 1:3-9:

Blessed be the God and Father of our Lord Jesus Christ! According to his great mercy, he has caused us to be born again to a living hope through the resurrection of Jesus Christ from the dead, to an inheritance that is imperishable, undefiled, and unfading, kept in heaven for you, who by God's power are being guarded through faith for a salvation ready to be revealed in time. In this you rejoice, though now for a little while, if necessary, you have been grieved by various trials, so that the tested genuineness of your faith—more precious than gold that perishes though it is tested by fire—may be found to result in praise and glory and honour at the revelation of Jesus Christ. Though you have not seen him, you love him. Though you do not now see him, you believe in him and rejoice with joy that is inexpressible and filled with glory, obtaining the outcome of your faith, the salvation of your souls.

You have a hope in the same way that you have an inheritance.

If I had a literal inheritance—that is, if my father had promised me that he would leave me a sum of money, and it had been written in a will and signed by a lawyer—that inheritance wouldn't depend on my state of mind. That inheritance wouldn't waver based on my belief in its existence or fade away because I worried about whether it was real.

In the same way, our inheritance in heaven—the promise of a safe and perfect relationship with God the Father, of life unending, of a place where there shall be no more mourning or crying or pain—doesn't depend on *how we feel*. Peter emphasizes this with a threefold repetition: "imperishable, undefiled, and unfading". And, as if that weren't enough, it is "kept in heaven for you". God's promises remain true even when our feelings waver.

This sort of hope is linked inextricably to joy.

We tend to think of joy as a synonym for happiness.

But this isn't the case in the Bible. Notice what Peter says: "rejoice, though now... you have been grieved".

How can you rejoice when you have been grieved?

By remembering your inheritance. And by gaining a joy that is far-sighted, able to see beyond the present emotion or situation. Joy is the partner of hope: the Spirit-given ability to see that this situation won't last and to see instead the promise of a kingdom that will never fade.

We are ultimately able to have this kind of joy and hope not by internal meditation or a kind of wishful thinking, but because of a person: because of Jesus, who "has caused us to be born again to a living hope through the resurrection".

The extraordinary reality of Jesus Christ being raised from the dead changes everything, and not even anxiety is immune to that reality.

How do you have hope within anxiety? Remind yourself of two things.

Firstly, anxiety won't last. The promise of heaven means that we have a heavenly inheritance, a life eternal, *free from anxiety*. Our life with God, basking in the security of a relationship with a Father who loves us—that life will far outweigh the troubles and stress of the life we live now.

Secondly, we can see the promises of heaven more vividly because of anxiety.

Anxiety can give us a relentless focus on all that we can't control.

And we have a promise that, in heaven, all these things will be turned around.

Anxiety rests upon foundations of uncertainty. And the resurrection of Jesus is a promise of something genuinely certain: that he will come again, that we will live again, and that a kingdom is coming: a kingdom built upon the foundations of a powerful God whose promises are true. A kingdom where there is no more crying and no more tears. A kingdom where we live a life of true freedom.

Conclusion

So what should we do?

Firstly, in God's kindness, he made this psalm small enough and sharp enough for you to hide it in your heart for when you need it. It would not be hard to write out the psalm, take a photo of it and use it as your phone wallpaper, put it on your fridge, or memorize it with a friend or Bible study group.

That's not to say this psalm is a magic mantra that you can recite to banish the spectre of anxiety. But you can take it as God's true word reminding you of those things that are always true: that God is good, and that his goodness is bigger than your anxiety. Therefore, you can find calm, and you (and others) can have hope.

Secondly, I hope this gives you permission—if you need it—to share your story with those who long to hear it.

Share your story not as a victim of anxiety but as a

child of hope, who, despite anxiety, is able to rest in the goodness of God. A person able to look to the place where we will be anxious no more.

Do you want to know the truth? The truth is that this book *might not help*, and that's okay. I've read a lot of books on anxiety and depression and mental health; some have helped more than others, and none has been the absolute cure. It would be particularly unhelpful to think that this book is different.

But as much as anything helps, be reminded of God's word one more time.

Have you ever thought about how, in relation to eternity, God gives us a very small, defined present in which to reside?

That is why Jesus' teaching is so brilliant. In Matthew 6, he reminds his listeners to not be anxious —but not by commanding them, "Look, just stop being anxious!" Instead, he reminds them to look at the birds and the flowers. So consider for a moment the immeasurable gifts that God has given you. Your body. Your breath flowing in and out of your lungs. Your ability to see these words on a page.

And then consider what else God has given you. Think of the heavenly Father who knows you so well. Who knows your every anxiety, doubt, fear, sorrow, and pain.

And who loves you anyway—enough to send his Son to walk through the valley, and show us the way home to eternal rest and peace.

Dear Father,
You are good.
Your goodness is bigger than my anxiety.
And so I can be calm.
I can trust in you.
And we can have hope.
Amen.

Author's note

Even for a short book like this, the list of people who have offered thoughts, prayers, and encouragement is long. I'm beyond thankful to have so many people on my side, including those I've forgotten to mention!

Thanks to Roger Bray for inviting me to give the talk that would become the first draft of this book, and to the saints at Newtown Erskineville Anglican Church for listening and encouraging me that I was on the right path.

Thanks to Ingrid Peters and Lauren Errington for psychological terms, fact-checking, and insights. Thanks to Matt Aroney, Katherine Cole, Mikey Bayliss and Rebecca Jee, who helped with feedback at various stages of the draft. Thanks to Kim Gibson and Jo van der Avoort, whose paper and talks respectively helped to illuminate this topic.

Thanks to everyone at Matthias Media, especially Ian Carmichael and Geoff Robson for patient and excellent editorial feedback.

And I dedicate this book to Mary—thank you for loving me and being a model of what it is to "hope in the LORD".

Feedback on this resource

We really appreciate getting feedback about our resources —not just suggestions for how to improve them, but also positive feedback and ways they can be used. We especially love to hear that the resources may have helped someone in their Christian growth.

You can send feedback to us via the 'Feedback' menu in our online store, or write to us at info@matthiasmedia.com.au.

Notes

1   B Bandelow and S Michaelis, 'Epidemiology of anxiety disorders in the 21st century', *Dialogues in Clinical Neuroscience*, 2015, 17(3):327-335, p 327, doi:10.31887/DCNS.2015.17.3/bbandelow. See also Anxiety & Depression Association of America, *Facts & Statistics*, ADAA website, 2021. adaa.org/understanding-anxiety/facts-statistics

2   H Ritchie and M Roser, 'Anxiety disorders', *Mental Health*, Our World in Data website, 2018. ourworldindata.org/mental-health#anxiety-disorders

3   Beyond Blue, *Statistics*, Beyond Blue website, 2021. beyondblue.org.au/media/statistics

4   This is not to say that if you have no choices, then you will have no anxiety at all—quite the opposite: sometimes, the most anxious times in our lives are when we feel things are completely out of our control, and when we have no choice.

5   See B Schwartz, *The Paradox of Choice: Why More is Less*, Harper Collins, 2009, pp 1-2.

6   See, for example, Deuteronomy 31:6, John 14:2 and 1 John 4:9-10.

7   R Alter, *The Book of Psalms: A Translation with Commentary*, WW Norton, 2007, p 458.

❀matthiasmedia

Matthias Media is an evangelical publishing ministry that seeks to persuade all Christians of the truth of God's purposes in Jesus Christ as revealed in the Bible, and equip them with high-quality resources, so that by the work of the Holy Spirit they will:

- abandon their lives to the honour and service of Christ in daily holiness and decision-making
- pray constantly in Christ's name for the fruitfulness and growth of his gospel
- speak the Bible's life-changing word whenever and however they can—in the home, in the world and in the fellowship of his people.

Our wide range of resources includes Bible studies, books, training courses, tracts and children's material. To find out more, and to access samples and free downloads, visit our website:

www.matthiasmedia.com

How to buy our resources

1. Direct from us over the internet:
   - in the US: www.matthiasmedia.com
   - in Australia: www.matthiasmedia.com.au
2. Direct from us by phone: please visit our website for current phone contact information.
3. Through a range of outlets in various parts of the world. Visit **www.matthiasmedia.com/contact** for details about recommended retailers in your part of the world.
4. Trade enquiries can be addressed to:
   - in the US and Canada: sales@matthiasmedia.com
   - in Australia and the rest of the world: sales@matthiasmedia.com.au

Register at our website for our **free** regular email update to receive information about the latest new resources, **exclusive special offers**, and free articles to help you grow in your Christian life and ministry.

How to Read the Bible Better

Richard Chin

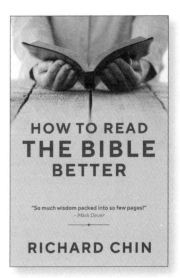

No matter how you feel about the world's bestselling book, we can all use a guiding hand to help us make the most of our Bible reading. In this short, readable book, pastor and preacher Richard Chin offers you a step-by-step guide to better Bible reading: how to make sense of the Scriptures, how to avoid the most common pitfalls, and how to let God's word shape your life.

"Richard's writing is always wonderfully clear and straightforward, and this work is no exception. This is a great resource to put into the hands of disciplers, new Christians, and, really, any church member looking to grow in the faith."— **Kevin DeYoung**

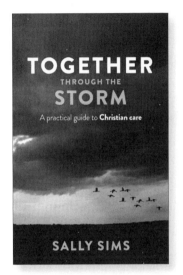